The History of the Telephone

Elizabeth Raum

Heinemann
LIBRARY

www.heinemann.co.uk/library
Visit our website to find out more information about Heinemann Library books.

To order:
 Phone 44 (0)1865 888066
 Send a fax to 44 (0)1865 314091
 Visit the Heinemann Bookshop at www.heinemann.co.uk/library to browse our catalogue and order online.

First published in Great Britain by Heinemann Library, Halley Court, Jordan Hill, Oxford OX2 8EJ, part of Harcourt Education.
Heinemann is a registered trademark of Harcourt Education Ltd.

Editorial: Kristen Truhlar and Diyan Leake
Design: Victoria Bevan and Tower Designs Ltd
Picture research: Mica Brancic
Production: Julie Carter

Origination: Dot Gradations
Printed and bound in China by South China Printing Co. Ltd

ISBN 978 0 431 19149 2
12 11 10 09 08
10 9 8 7 6 5 4 3 2 1

British Library Cataloguing in Publication Data
Raum, Elizabeth
The history of the telephone. - (Inventions that changed the world)
1. Telephone - History - Juvenile literature 2. Telephone - Social aspects - Juvenile literature
I. Title
303.4'833

ISBN-13: 9780431191492

Acknowledgements
The publishers would like to thank the following for permission to reproduce photographs: p. **4** Corbis/Hulton-Deutsch Collection, p. **5** Corbis/Bettman, p. **6** Getty Images/Time Life Pictures/Mansell/Time Life Pictures, p. **7** Corbis/Bettmann, p. **8** Corbis/E R Morse (Photos12), p. **9** Getty Images/Time Life Pictures/Mansell, p. **10** Science & Society/Science Museum, p. **11** Science & Society/Science Museum, p. **12** Mary Evans Picture Library/Corbis, p. **13** Science & Society/Science Museum, p. **14** Corbis/Bettman, p. **15** Corbis/Dick Lemen, p. **16** Mary Evans Picture Library, p. **17** Corbis/Stefano Bianchetti, p. **18** Getty Images/Hulton Archive, p. **19** Corbis/Hulton-Deutsch Collection, p. **20** Getty Images/Retrofile/H. Armstrong Roberts, p. **21** Science & Society/Science Museum, p. **22** Getty Images/Hulton Archive, p. **23** Science Photo Library/NASA, p. **24** Corbis/Ted Soqui, p. **25** Photolibrary.com, p. **26** Getty Images, p. **27** Photolibrary.com.

Cover photograph reproduced with permission of Getty Images/Hulton Archive/Three Lions.

Every effort has been made to contact copyright holders of any material reproduced in this book. Any omissions will be rectified in subsequent printings if notice is given to the publishers.

Contents

Before telephones. 4

"Mr Watson, come here!" .6

Telephone bells. 8

Bell sells phones. 10

Phone services and directories 12

"Please connect me..." 14

Calling long distances 16

Dial it yourself 18

Making telephones better. 20

Satellites help out 22

Mobile phones 24

How telephones changed life 26

Timeline. 28

World map activity 29

Find out more. 30

Glossary 31

Index. 32

Some words are shown in bold, **like this**. You can find out what they mean by looking in the glossary.

Before telephones

Before there were telephones, the only way to speak to someone who was not close by was to shout. If friends or family lived far away, the only way to speak to them was to visit them or to send a letter. Visiting or sending letters could take many days.

Before telephones, people who lived far away had no way to call for help.

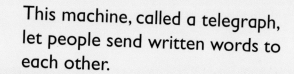
This machine, called a telegraph, let people send written words to each other.

In 1844 an **inventor** in the United States named Samuel Morse **invented** the **telegraph**. The telegraph let people send words over a wire. But they could only send written words, not their voices.

"Mr Watson, come here!"

Alexander Graham Bell wanted to make a talking **telegraph**. Bell was born in Scotland, but moved to the United States when he was a young man. In March of 1876, Bell was testing something new. He called it the telephone.

Alexander Graham Bell lived from 1847 to 1922.

The first telephone looked very different from telephones today.

Bell needed help and his helper, Thomas Watson, was in another room. Bell picked up his telephone and spoke into it. He said, "Mr Watson, come here!" Watson heard him even though he was not near by. They had **invented** the telephone.

Telephone bells

Bell and Watson showed people their telephone at a big fair. People were surprised to hear a voice on the telephone. Bell, Watson, and other **inventors** worked to make the telephone better.

Alexander Graham Bell showed his telephone to many people.

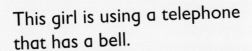
This girl is using a telephone that has a bell.

In 1878 Thomas Watson added a bell to the telephone. The bell told people that a call was coming in. Today telephones can ring, buzz, or play music when a call comes in.

Bell sells phones

In 1877 Alexander Graham Bell began the Bell Telephone Company to make and sell telephones. He wanted to begin a telephone **service** in the United States. This would let people make telephone calls to one another.

This newspaper ad told people about the Bell telephone.

HALF FULL SIZE

THE TELEPHONE.

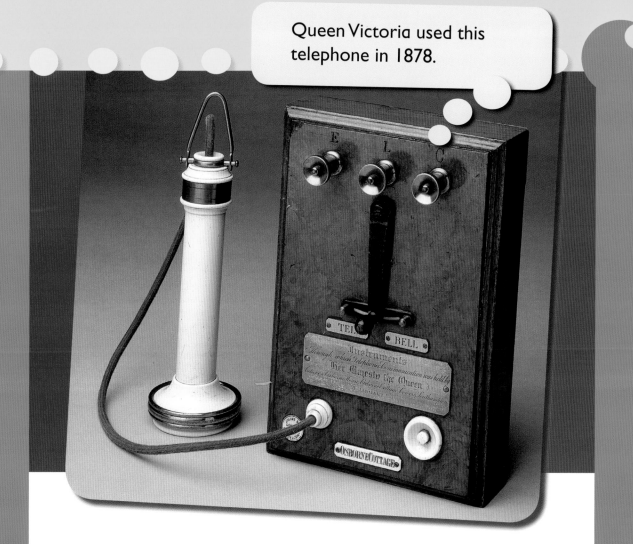

Queen Victoria used this telephone in 1878.

In 1878 Bell went to England. He spent a year talking to people about his telephone. He met with Queen Victoria and other important people. He talked them into starting a telephone service in England.

Phone services and directories

The first telephone **service** began in the United States in 1878. Twenty-one people signed up for service. At first, people did not buy the telephones. They **rented** them.

People used telephones in stores because it cost too much money to have a telephone.

PRESCRIPTIONS ACCURATELY DISPENSED

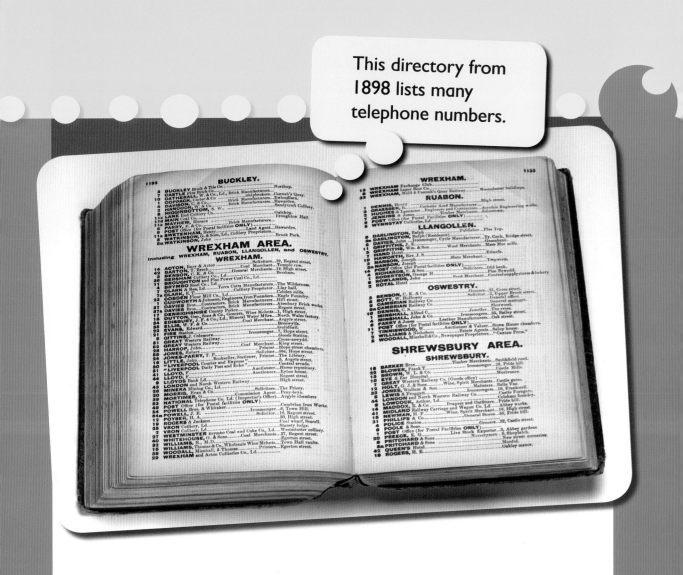

This directory from 1898 lists many telephone numbers.

Telephone companies put out a list of phone numbers, called a **directory**. The first directory appeared in 1878. Early phone numbers used letters. Later on, they changed to numbers to make dialling easier.

"Please connect me..."

To make a telephone call, a person called the telephone company office. Someone there, called an **operator**, would **connect** the caller to another telephone. The first operators were young men. Soon many women became operators.

By 1880 most telephone operators were women.

At first, every phone had its own wire connecting it to the telephone company. The wires were carried on telephone poles. Later, the wires were twisted together into a thick rope called a **cable**. The cables looked better than the wires.

The first telephone poles had many wires.

Calling long distances

Calls between states or countries are called **long-distance** calls. By 1884 it was possible to call long distance between the cities of Boston and New York. By 1891 people in England could call people in Europe. An **operator connected** the calls.

This girl is using a telephone in 1905.

In 1892 Alexander Graham Bell made a long-distance telephone call from New York to Chicago.

It took time to put up telephone poles. By 1892 people could call from New York City to Chicago. By 1915 people could call from New York City to San Francisco, in California. Soon people could make long-distance calls everywhere.

Dial it yourself

In 1919 **inventors** made a telephone with a dial. People did not need to go through an **operator** to make a call. They could call someone by dialling the number themselves.

This man is using the dial on the telephone to make a call.

Telephone tables had a place for a telephone on top and a directory below.

Telephone companies had to change from operators to a new way of **connecting** calls. This change took many years. By 1950 most people had changed to dial telephones.

Making telephones better

Touch-tone telephones use buttons instead of dials. The first touch-tone telephone was **invented** in 1941. **Inventors** kept making them better. In 1963 people could buy touch-tone telephones.

Touch-tone telephones are easier to use than dial telephones.

The first answering machines were big. They were **connected** to the telephone with a wire.

An inventor in Denmark named Valdemar Poulsen made the first telephone **answering machine** in 1898. Other inventors worked to make it better. The first answering machines for home telephones were not sold until 1971.

Satellites help out

People looked for ways to make **long-distance** calls better. Sometimes it was hard for people to hear each other during these calls. Sometimes people had to dial a call several times before it was **connected**.

Sometimes buzzing sounds made it hard to hear over the telephone.

The *Telstar I* satellite helped make long-distance telephone calls better.

In 1962 a **satellite** called *Telstar I* was sent into space. It was the first **telecommunication** satellite. Better satellites followed. Thanks to satellites, long-distance service got better.

Mobile phones

Telephones were first used in trucks and police cars in 1946. In 1973 a man in the United States named Martin Cooper **invented** the **mobile** phone. It did not need to be **connected** to wires to make calls. Today more than a billion people all over the world use mobile phones.

Martin Cooper invented the mobile phone. The first mobiles were big.

Inventors have made smaller and better mobile phones. In 2000 the first phone with a camera in it was invented. These phones can take pictures. Mobile phones can also play music and games.

Today mobile phones can do many things. This girl is using a camera phone to take a picture.

How telephones changed life

Before telephones, people had to travel to speak to someone. People had to send letters to stay in touch. Today telephones let people call family and friends anytime they want to.

Today telephones help families and friends keep in touch with each other.

Mobile phones are everywhere around us.

Today telephones are everywhere. People take telephones with them when they travel. Telephones are in cars, homes, schools, shops, and many other places.

Timeline

1876 Alexander Graham Bell **invents** the telephone.

1878 Telephone service begins in the state of Connecticut in the United States.

1884 **Long-distance** service begins.

1898 Valdemar Poulsen invents the **answering machine**.

1915 Long-distance service begins between the states of New York and California.

1919 First dial telephone is invented.

1946 Telephones are used in trucks and police cars.

1962 *Telstar I* **satellite** is sent into space.

1963 **Touch-tone** telephones are for sale.

1971 Home answering machines are for sale.

1973 Martin Cooper invents the **mobile** phone.

2000 Camera phone is invented.

World map activity

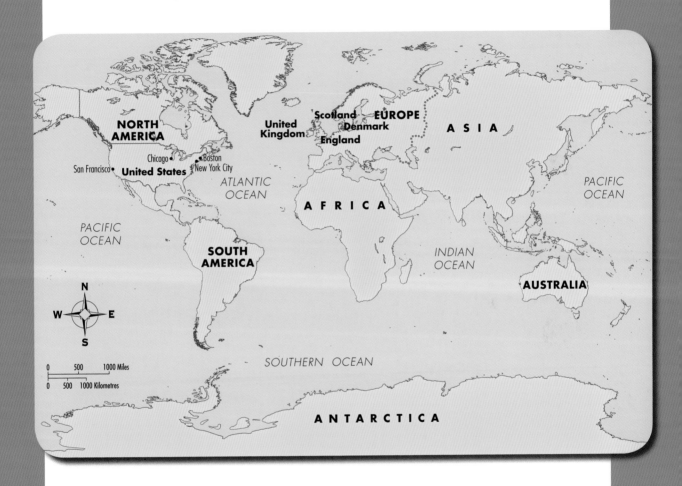

The countries talked about in this book are labelled on this world map. Try to find each **inventor**'s country on the map.

Find out more

Books

Alexander Graham Bell: Inventor of the Telephone, John Micklos, Jr (HarperCollins, 2006).

Household History: Telephones, Elaine Marie Alphin (Carolrhoda, 2001).

Inventing the Telephone, Erinn Banting (Crabtree, 2006).

Websites

FCC Kids Zone - Telephone History
http://www.fcc.gov/cgb/kidszone/history.html

Enchanted Learning -
http://www.enchantedlearning.com/inventors

Technology at Home -
http://www.pbs.org/wgbh/aso/tryit/tech

Glossary

answering machine machine that records and plays telephone messages

cable many wires twisted together

connect put together

directory list of numbers or addresses

invent make something that did not exist before

inventor someone who makes something that did not exist before

long distance far away

mobile something that travels

operator person who helps connect telephone calls

rent pay money to use something for a while

satellite machine put into space that helps make calls better

service something a company does for people

telecommunication talking over a distance by telephone

telegraph machine that sends words over a wire

touch-tone telephone telephone that uses buttons instead of a dial

Index

answering machines   21

Bell, Alexander Graham
   6-7, 8, 10-11, 17
Bell Telephone Company   10

camera phones   25
connecting calls   14-15, 16,
   19, 22, 24
Cooper, Martin   24

Denmark   21
dial telephones   18-19
dialling calls   18, 22
directories   13

England   11, 16

long-distance calls   16-17,
   22-23

mobile telephones   24-25
Morse, Samuel   5

operators   14, 16, 19

Poulsen, Valdemar   21

Queen Victoria   11

renting telephones   12

Scotland   6
sending letters   4, 26

telegraph   5, 6
telephone bells   9
telephone company   10, 13,
   14-15
telephone poles   15, 17
telephone service   10-11, 12
Telstar I satellite   23
touch-tone telephones   20

United States   5, 6, 10, 12

Watson, Thomas   7, 8-9, 10
wires   5, 15, 24